Content

FOREWORD

Kathleen watched a TV programme in the 1970's which showed James Walters doing some crochet in a very free way. This inspired her to write to the broadcasting company to ask if there were any crochet courses where she could learn to crochet. Their reply resulted in her attending the first of five Summer Schools on Crochet held by the Lancaster and Morecambe College of Further Education where I was a full-time lecturer. Whatever aspects were covered during the five days of the course one year, resulted in an amazing array of crocheted items to be displayed for comment on the following year. Those who were privileged to see these designs felt it would be a sad loss to the crochet world if they were unavailable for others to see. Unfortunately whilst all this excitement was going on, crochet was still thought of as the 'parson's nose' of textiles making it difficult to show them to the world at large. In addition Kathleen would not let her work be seen unless it was perfect and no amount of urging could persuade her that her achievements were more than mediocre.

Ten years later I am delighted to be instrumental in bringing that talent to the notice of all crochet enthusiasts everywhere, even if I did have to turn Crochet Design into a publishing company to do it!

The garments included in "The Appeal of Crochet" were inspired in many different ways and cover approximately three years of exploration and experimentation with texture and colour. They are in chronological order to allow other adventurers of the crochet hook to follow the 'nature trail' pioneered by Kathleen during this period. With her botanical background, I use the phrase 'nature trail' deliberately.

The first part of the book covers the way in which it all happened and with few exceptions they are the memories and processes as recalled by Kathleen. The second part of the book covers a variety of details which will help you complete any ideas of your own based on the suggestions within these pages.

Pauline Turner

INTRODUCTION

What this book is.

1. It is a diary following on from "Exploring Crochet"

2. It is full of inspiration, heartaches, laughter and achievement.

3. It is a source of how to find your own creative joys as well as being infinitely practical.

4. It is full of colour and texture.

5. It is a reference book full of up to date practical skills, with new ways of using the hook, and new ways to cheat.

6. It is a human interest book giving confidence to all who read it.

7. It is what crochet is in the 1990's [although the work contained in these pages was produced from 1979-1983]

What this book is not!

1. This book is not a book of crochet patterns and yet it describes how to produce the designs illustrated.

2. This book is not a book on crochet techniques and yet it inevitably contains techniques.

3. This book is not a book of rules and regulations, but rather how to enjoy crochet using whatever method fits to achieve your ideas.

CHAPTER ONE

SNOWFLAKES IN SUMMER

If you are fortunate enough to be taught how to crochet by inspired and inspiring teachers, as I was, you discover, almost as soon as you have made your first row of chain stitches and worked a few rows of basic stitches into it, that not only is it a singularly easy craft to practise but it offers enormous scope for a beginner to develop creatively.

You notice, from observation of your first tentative efforts how much the choice of yarns affects the appearance of a fabric worked in simple, basic stitches. If you have at your disposal a range of hook sizes and yarns of different thickness, texture and colour you find, by experiment (or "doodling") that you can combine them to express an idea or a theme imaginatively, almost from the word "go", using only the most basic techniques.

The main fabric of the jacket I called "Snowflakes in Summer" illustrates this point. It is worked entirely in chain stitches and double crochet but uses many different yarns.

It was begun on a brief bank holiday in May - and all but the waist-bands, wrist bands, borders and buttons were finished in those few days. We had hoped to spend our time enjoying spring sunshine out of doors, playing in the garden and walking in the woods with four of our grandchildren and their parents. However, on the first morning of our visit we woke up to see snow falling heavily in huge soft flakes all over the spring blossom and the young green leaves. Already the snow lay several inches deep on the lawn but was too wet for playing snowballs. It was, nevertheless, a most beautiful as well as surprising scene.

But how should we and the children, whose ages ranged between three and ten years old, amuse ourselves? We stood at the window and watched the strange blurring and blending of all the lovely greens and white blossom and snow,

and I wondered if we could not capture this image in a textile and perhaps perpetuate the memory of it. We wasted no more time but got into the car and drove to the splendid wool shop near my daughter's home which, fortunately stayed open at holiday times and weekends. What fun we had searching for all kinds of green yarns - mohair, boucle, chenille, chunky and DDK and DK yarns and one white knoppy yarn -the knops were very soft and fat and shaped exactly like the large snowflakes still falling outside. Before leaving the shop with our treasure-trove of yarns we checked we had a complete range of hook sizes to work them with.

As soon as we got home, after warming ourselves up with hot drinks and food we started, as one always starts, with some experimental "doodling", trying out hooks and yarns first of all by working lengths of chain stitches, which even the three-year old who had never previously held a crochet hook in his hand soon learned to do enthusiastically.

"Doodling", though it can be fun, is an indispensable and essentially serious exercise from which one learns how to produce a fabric which will suit the purpose and how to achieve "special effects" - whatever is desired. Sometimes you find you have to spend several days on these exercises before you find answers to your questions, but such time is never wasted. Fortunately we found answers to our 'Snowflakes in Summer' questions quite quickly. The snow was falling vertically on this windless day and it was this gentle movement I wanted to catch. This required that the fabric should be worked in vertical rather than horizontal rows, and we found that the downward movement could be expressed by using lengths of chain stitches, side by side in close proximity and each one simply attached to the previous chain at evenly spaced intervals by double crochet, 1dc for thicker yarns and 1dc, 1ch, 1dc for the thinner yarns. The "snowflakes" were incorporated by carrying the white knoppy yarn above a row worked in DK on the right side of the fabric and catching it in at every joining position with a single dc worked over it in the DK yarn, in other words, it was woven in, and the knops left well raised on the surface. The size and spacing of the knops determined the length of the chain between each joining point. The number of stitches in each length of chain varied according to the thickness of the yarn and hook size used. It was, of course, essential to check at the completion of every new row that the length of the chain between the joins corresponded exactly to that of the chain in the previous row and every preceeding row, carefully avoiding any puckering (too many chains or too large a hook) or pulling (too few chains or too small a hook) so that, as the fabric developed it would lie perfectly flat. It was necessary therefore that the final "doodle" performed before proceeding to work on the actual fabric should display all the yarns to their best advantage and they should be arranged so that each one enhanced the character and colour of its neighbours and furthermore produce a light, supple fabric which, when placed on a flat surface, formed a regular rectangle with absolutely straight edges. Only then could the correct tension be estimated.

I tried "doodling" on a base of chain - one chain of 31sts (a multiple of 5 and 6 plus 1) and another of 43sts (a multiple of 6 and 7 plus 1) For these chains I used a 4.50mm hook and worked a first row into the shorter chain as follows:

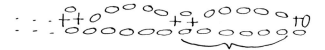

Chain base multiple of 5

Chain base multiple of 6

and the longer chain and first row similarly, but with different spacing then placed the knopped yarn over each sample to establish which spacing would display the snowflakes in relief and suggest the steady rhythm of their fall.

Once this point was decided I completed my first strip using each type of yarn at least once, then I turned the sample round and began working again on the other side of the foundation chain.

My final and most satisfactory "doodle" suggested that the fabric could be used to make a softly draping, bat-wing jacket, worked in two sections, left and right, in mirror-image.

A measurement was taken straight over the shoulder from top of waist at back to top of waist at front, and the foundation chain worked very slightly longer than this measurement and in accordance with the selected multiple of stitches plus one. I worked a straight strip on one side of the foundation chain until it was wide enough just to cover the shoulder from the point where the initial measurement was taken and meet, when folded in half, at the sides underneath the arms.

I marked a position a few inches from either end, leaving a short space for the side seams and rejoined the yarn and worked between these points and began the sleeves, gradually decreasing at the sides to slope towards the wrists.

The work was then turned round and restarted on the other side of the foundation chain, carrying out shaping at front and back neck respectively. The underarm seams and side seams were joined and the wrist band worked in raised treble ribbing in DK yarn into the edge stitches of the main fabric. Similar raised treble ribbing was used for the wrist bands and finally a button, button-hole border worked all round the front edges and back neck, and buttons made in the same DK yarn, using a much finer hook, 2.50mm or 3.00mm for a very firm fabric.

CHAPTER TWO

OWL AND FLOWERS COAT

An idea can come from a single source, an impression of a summer garden in the snow, for example, as already described, or it can develop, bit by bit from several quite different sources.

The "Owl and Flowers" coat began when I was learning how to work bullion stitches. It required much practice before I got the knack and, since I prefer to make my exercises in technical skills as interesting and enjoyable as possible, I tried working them in circles round a small crochet ring centre instead of in rows which can be very boring. The bullion stitches began to look like the petals of flowers, such flowers as I had seen carved in relief on stone screens and ornamental panels in churches; and I remembered working a bullion stitch flower motif previously so I let this one grow, as all my crochet grows, from exploratory "doodles".

About this time I was also experimenting with natural dyes, and for this I had acquired a large supply of undyed Welsh DK wool, mostly spun from white fleeces but some from black. Using leaves and twigs, elderberries and blackberries and several different mordants I was able to produce a surprisingly varied range of gold, green, brown, pink and purple shades. When the dyed skeins were hung up to dry we noticed how beautifully all these colours blended together, and how different mordants affected not only the colour but the texture of the wool and I began to get excited about using them for my bullion stitch flowers in every possible permutation.

One great advantage that natural dyes have over commercial dyes is that there is never any risk of colour clash. The contrasts are always gentle, subtle and harmonious, never dramatic, though when I made two flowers using the natural black wool for the centres and they were placed, quite by chance, side by side, they suddenly glared back at me like a pair of owl's eyes and I immediately thought of Alan Garner's book "The Owl Service" and of the old Welsh legend on which it was based which tells how the magicians made a lovely girl, a goddess, from the blossoms of oak, broom and meadow-sweet, and called her Blodeuwedd, then turned her into an owl as a punishment for betraying the husband they had made her for.

So it was that the bullion stitches, the many coloured wools, the flowers and the owl motif began to come together and combine in a single theme.

I scattered my flowers, now varying in size and structure as well as colour, on the floor, juggled with them a bit until they arranged themselves, not in predetermined patterns, but rather as wild flowers arrange themselves in summer fields to display themselves to bees and butterflies and other pollinating agents. Then I began filling the spaces between with little bits of gold, green, light and darker browns and creamy pink - all of them natural-looking meadow colours.

I joined the owl eyes and made a beak between them, and then worked his soft, pale, cream feathered breast and his brown wings and set his claws on a cluster of flowers shining out of the dark cavities in the trees. Then I surrounded him with green leaves.

It was only when these large "doodles" were almost completed that I thought I could use them for the front panels and the back of a full length coat, for I still had plenty of dyed wool in reserve.

Once this idea took hold I had to plan the work in a more disciplined way. The main challenge was how to maintain a sufficiently interesting variation of texture and colour in the skirt and sleeves. The finished garment had to fit well and hang well and hold its shape without resorting to a lining which invariably tends to stiffen the fabric. Much of the beauty peculiar to crochet lies in its suppleness, in the way it drapes, moves and almost flows, without losing stability. These sections also had to play a supporting role for the owl and flower motifs on the bodice, but they must not look "plodding" or dull, so I kept in mind the image of a field in summer where the meadow-sweet might grow. Bullion stitch flowers were used only at the top of the skirt and near the edges of the sleeves but now restricted in formal rows like flowers planted in the border of a garden, drilled like a row of soldiers.

When the coat was finished I gave it to a lovely young girl much kinder than Blodeuwedd. It happened that she was very unhappy about this time so I thought the story could be turned round and the owl coat help to transform my sad little friend into a happy girl of flowers.

It is twelve years since I made this coat and the colours have faded. The leaves surrounding the owl have lost their rich summer green and now look pale and autumnal. Nevertheless, I believe this coat is still worn with pleasure and I still like looking at it if only because it has so many happy associations. It reminds me of another little girl, the mischievous eleven-year-old granddaughter, Helena, who stayed with us during that summer and helped me to collect all the plant materials and to dye the wool. When she got tired of boiling bits of vegetation and wool, she would leave the steamy kitchen and refresh herself by turning cartwheels in the garden. During one such interlude a passing neighbour stopped to speak to her, asking, "And how is your granny today, dear?" to which Helena replied with a big, cheerful smile: "Oh, Granny is dyeing in the kitchen", and blithely continued doing cartwheels. Fortunately her grandfather overheard this brief conversation and was able to explain matters to our kindly but somewhat perturbed neighbour.

It is the same, but now grown-up Helena who models the coat. I'm pleased to say that she has kept her quick wits and her lively, sometimes mordant sense of humour.

Mordants used for dyeing the yarn used in the Owl and Flowers Coat
1. Alum
2. Dichromate of potash
3. Copper Sulphate
4. Potassium Aluminium Sulphate
5. Stannous Chloride (Tin) and Cream of Tarter
6. Ferrous Sulphate

CHAPTER THREE

SUMMER MEADOW

While Bernat Klein was still designing his wonderful textiles and having them woven at his mill in Galashiels he allowed me to buy some of the mohair he had had specially dyed for him. Among them there was one that brought to mind all the pale and gentle colours and subtly varied textures - feathery, velvety, silky - of tall flowering meadow grasses in the late summer.

There are few things I enjoy doing more on a beautiful summer day than to stand and watch as the wind flows through long meadow grass, swaying it this way and that so that the colours change as in watered silk, from pale gold to pale pink, to silver, to silver-green, to darker green, to light brown, to creamy beige.

I wondered if it would be possible to construct a textile which could reproduce an illusion, an impression, of this lovely movement using the Bernat Klein yarn which had made me think of meadow grass.

I visualised a full length cape, falling in waves to a wide scalloped lower edge, and the fabric having the softness, the fluidity, the gently way-ward movement of the various flowering grasses - fescues; silvery hair-grass; wavy hair-grass, which looks like a pink mist, and lustrous, velvety, pink-flushed "Yorkshire Fog"- all common grasses which you can find not only in meadows but along unsprayed un-mown road sides, such as those where I played as a child, under a bright blue sky where larks sang from early morning till sunset. I wanted to evoke a whole remembered world.

It took many hours and days of "doodling" before I produced any sample which seemed to offer possibilities of further development. When you are working "from scratch" you can only see what you want to do when you have done it! It is important to remember this otherwise you can become discouraged by what can seem fruitless effort, a deplorable waste of time and material (for mohair does not unravel easily and may well be damaged in the process) producing nothing but frustration.

Eventually, a simple modification of a wave stitch pattern worked in dtr raised to the front on the right side and to the back on the wrong side, using a size 10.00mm hook began to look promising; however, I had to work a fairly large sample, a dozen rows or more over two repeats of the pattern, (each pattern a multiple of 26 stitches for the bottom of the cape) before I could see a way to suggest some idea of waving meadow grass. After this the work flowed easily and quickly.

The cape is made in one piece, including the collar, and there are only 34 rows! I used 800gm of the Bernat Klein mohair, but the quantity may vary with a different quality of mohair as I discovered when I made a cape suggestive of the young spring wheat, with waves of silver-green. I have summarised the instructions which are, in fact, very simple to follow once you have a clear idea of what you are doing. If you work the sample illustrated in the diagram you will quickly recognise the "troughs" and "crests" of the waves. Tension is not vitally important since the cape is not "fitted", but I made a tension sample in dc, using the 10.00mm hook and found that 14sts and 16 rows in dc produced a square = 20cm x 20cm.

Most of the cape was worked on the 10.00mm hook, but hook sizes 9.00mm, 8.00mm, 7.00mm and 6.00mm were used also for shaping, as explained in the instructions, but I recommend that before beginning the main work the sample illustrated in the diagram is carried out. This will give you confidence to proceed.

Foundation Row for two repeats of wave pattern

ch 52 plus 4ch to turn. 1dtr in 5th ch from hook and in each next 10 ch, miss next ch, 1 dtr in next ch, miss next ch, 1 dtr in each of next 11ch, ch1, 1 dtr in next ch,ch1, 1dtr in each of next 11 ch, miss next ch, 1 dtr in next ch, miss next ch, 1 dtr in each of next 11 ch, ch1, 1 dtr in last ch. 4 ch to turn.

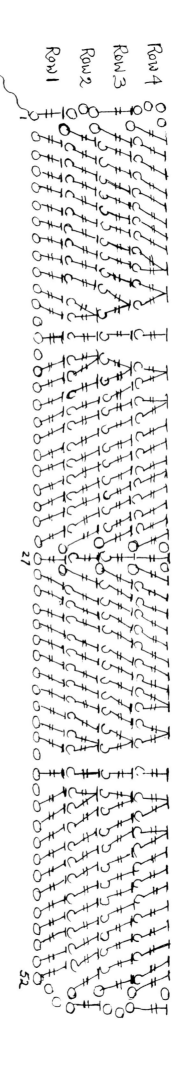

Diagram illustrates two repeats of the wave pattern.

The method of working decreasings for rows 6, 12, 18 and 22 is shown in Row 4 of sample below.

Instructions for Mohair cape

With 10.00mm hook make 160ch.

Row 1: With WS facing work as shown in sample diagram but with six repeats of the wave pattern instead of two.

Row 2: 4ch to turn, 1dtr in each ch, RdtrF round all dtr of Row 1 as described, giving you 6 multiples of 24sts plus 1st, [157sts].

Row 3: 4ch to turn, 1dtr in each ch, RdtrB round each Rdtr of previous row.

Continue straight until 5 rows have been completed.

Decreasings: On decrease rows work Rdtr2tog on either side of the regular decreases on each side of the "trough" in the wave pattern. See diagram. Keeping wave pattern continuous decrease on the following rows:

Row 6: gives 6 multiples of 24sts plus 1 which equals 145sts

Row 12: [133st]

Row 18: [121st]

Row 22: [109]

Change to 9.00mm hook on Row 23.

Row 24: [97st]

Change to 8.00mm hook on Row 25. Row 26: [85st]

Change to 7.00mm hook on Row 27, 1ch to turn.

Row 28: With RS facing gather waves as follows to produce a straight edge.

1dc in turning ch of Row 27, *4ch, miss 1ch, work 11 unfinished RdtrF round each of next 11sts, yoh, pull yarn through all 12 loops on hook to form a cluster, 3ch, miss 1ch, 1dc in next st [at the "crest" of the wave], rep from * 5 times, 1dc in last st, 1ch to turn. [55st].

Row 29: dc to end, [55st]. A 6.00mm hook can be used for this row only, for extra firmness. 4ch to turn.

Row 30:[draw string row] miss 2sts, 1tr in next st, *1ch, miss 1st, 1tr in next st, rep from * to end, 1ch, turn.

Row 31: dc to end (55sts)

Collar

Note that collar shaping is carried out simply by changing the hook size on each of the 3 rows.

Row 32: Change to 8.00mm hook, 4ch, turn, (this becomes a WS row because the collar turns back over the cape at the neck edge), dtr to end [55st].

Row 33: 4ch to turn, 54RdtrF [55st]. Row 34: change to 10.00mm hook, 4ch to turn, 54RdtrB, [55st]. Fasten off.

To Complete

Spread the garment out on a flat surface so that the inside (WS) with its ridges are facing towards you to finish the edges at the sides of the cape and collar.Join yarn with slip stitch (ss) into first st of foundation chain at extreme left side edge at bottom of cape. Using hook size 6.00mm or 7.00mm 3ch 1ss under edge st of first ridge, 3ch 1ss under edge st of next ridge; cont up this side of cape to the neck. Check carefully that each chain corresponds exactly to the height of the stitch which lies beneath it. Work a similar row of ss and ch on right edge of cape. All sts will be invisible from RS. Work collar edges in the same way, that is,into the edges of ridges on the wrong side. This procedure will prevent any tendency for the fabric to sag. My cape retains its shape after ten or more years of wear.

Draw String: With 8.00mm hook and three strands of mohair work a chain approximately 180cm in length. Thread this through Row 30.

CHAPTER FOUR

"MARGUERITES"

My life-long love affair with plants began in early infancy when I could walk head-high with the tall summer grasses and the marguerites (ox-eye daisies). It was something - as much as possible - of this intensely enjoyable experience, when the grasses tickled my face and the clover, smelled so strongly and deliciously of honey, so much nearer to my nose than now, that I wanted to recover. "Marguerites" was an attempt to give substance to the ghost of a long-ago summer.

But the immediate starting point for the marguerite waistcoat was a soft focus photograph of these big daisies, almost life-size, set against a deliberately out-of-focus background of misty green grasses which I found, by chance on the back cover of a book. It was a highly evocative image which seemed to echo and link with an indelible childhood memory and its expansive spectrum of sensations, all the visual and tactile excitements and delights associated with first getting to know the world.

I began by making a collection of yarns, choosing colours and textures with great care because it was important that all the elements of the finished work should both look and feel right, satisfying to the touch as well as to the eye. I chose a smooth DK yarn, a pussy-willow colour for the basic waistcoat which was made first. I used a fine white mohair for the large ray-florets of the daisy and a grey-green brushed wool together with a yellow unbrushed mohair (the tiny loops of which looked exactly like a dusting of pollen) for the central mass of tiny disc florets. I found a deeper shade of grey-green, more green than grey for the backs, buds and stems of flowers. I chose a silver-grey chunky yarn for the thistles (basal leaves only) and a very fine, silky, but not too fluffy mohair for the weeds and their seed-pods. (See chapter 13 for instructions for making motifs)

My idea was to create the illusion of being in the field and of looking at the marguerites from every angle. I wanted to see them, not only as they faced me but also as, more often, they looked up to the sun. I wanted to see them from the back as they turned over and I wanted to represent them at every stage of development from the tight bud to the fully opened flower. I wanted the leaves and stems to curve and twist, and I wanted to show everything in high relief, emerging from an understated background.

I had to experiment with all the techniques I had ever learned, select the most promising and set about finding ways to modify them to suit my requirements. Techniques, such as the construction of clones-knots, traditionally used in Irish lace crochet and worked with a very fine yarn and a very fine hook, look very different when made with a fine, silky mohair and using a much larger hook, and could suggest fat seed-pods.

Patterns originally devised for making braid trimmings could be adapted to suggest the crinkled leaves of thistles. Confidence to play freely and adventurously on old themes in this way comes, ultimately, from good teaching methods. It is from "doodling" in stimulating crochet work-shops that you best learn how to think imaginatively in crochet and invent your own motifs. Whatever you do with your hook and your yarn, something happens. It may not be what you wanted to happen but, sooner or later, serendipity sets in. Once again I would point out that you only find out what it is you want to do when you have done it!

Slowly through many trials and errors, I built up a collection of motifs, grasses and weeds as well as marguerites. I tried out various arrangements, both on the fronts and back of the waistcoat and when the arrangement corresponded, as nearly as I could make, to my part-remembered, part-imagined, part-real, part fairy-tale field, I stitched the motifs in position. I made daisy-bud buttons and threaded them through chain loops to hold the edge-to-edge jacket together at the front. I worked in crab stitch all round the jacket and sleeve openings, this finish being more consistent with the impression of an "out-of-focus" blurred background than well defined borders.

CHAPTER FIVE

"IRISES"

"Irises" began in quite a different way from "Marguerites" and was attempted in response to a suggestion (and challenge) proposed by a dear friend in crochet, Sylvia Cosh. She presented me with a post-card reproduction of a detail from one of Claude Monet's paintings of his water-garden at Giverny. "Now then", she said, "crochet this!"

I could see the sumptuous greenery, the tall, graceful leaf blades of the reeds and pliant rushes rising up from the pond and its boggy surroundings in almost unbroken continuity and, here and there among them, bewitching glimpses of water-irises.

Monet's Irises, like all his water-garden paintings, represents part of a real garden, a garden he made himself, but the representations extend beyond realism and it is to his communication of intensely excited vision that we respond so strongly emotionally. We feel as if we had been invited to take a walk in Eden. We feel the stillness of the garden, yet sense it is full of movement, for it is a fluid world of ever-changing light and shade - an equivocal world, nature seen through a magic prism.

During the summer of 1953 while I was stranded in Paris for three weeks because of a transport strike, I took advantage of the situation and spent many hours in front of the series Waterlilies, and went day after day to stand and look at the great panels by Monet in the Orangerie. I got to know these paintings very well. Sylvia's post-card was, for me, like a tiny window through which I could see just one small part of that most magical and most mysterious of gardens, where one can recognise all the plants though none of them are ever quite in focus, they almost dissolve in incandescent light.

I learned more about crochet and more about colour from my struggles with "Irises" than from any other experiment in crochet. While working on it I had to distance myself as much as possible from every-day distractions; there were so many diabolically difficult problems to tackle simultaneously.

The water-garden paintings which occupied most of the last twenty years of the artist's life are, in many respects, unlike any of his previous series, Haystacks, Poplars, Views of London, Views of Venice and Rouen Cathedral, though, of course, these also were attempts to render light at different times of day and in different seasons. In common with other Impressionist painters, Monet sought to render atmospheric vibrancy by juxtaposition of very small, distinct brush strokes of pure colour. If you stand close up to any of these paintings you come face to face with an incomprehensible mess and muddle of paint - but stand back and everything becomes clear, sparkling and quivering with life.

In "Marguerites" the basic waistcoat was made first, it was the "canvas" for my picture, though not an inert surface. But the "Irises" waistcoat was built up, one row at a time from the foundation chain at the bottom of the waistband. Before beginning this project I searched the mills as well as the wool shops for as many different shades of green and blue and iris-colours as I could distinguish from careful observation of the post-card, and found them in mohair, boucle and slubbed yarn and in 4-ply wool.

Making the Fabric

The 4 ply wool was always used working two strands together, each of a different green, and changing at least one of the two colours at the beginning of every new row, and sometimes changing the colours within the row. I used this double thickness of 4 ply with a bulky slubbed yarn in gentian blue flecked with green (another Bernat Klein yarn) for making the waistband.

The slubbed yarn was approximately the same thickness as the two strands of 4 ply and it was, therefore, possible to alternate them at any desired position along the row, working double crochet over the yarn not in use and carrying it along ready for changing at any selected position in the row. By this method it was possible to avoid any solid patches of colour since the colours were in a constant process of change and interchange, giving a more natural, liquid appearance to my "pond" and its trembling reflections. Nothing changes colour so quickly as water.

I lost count of the number of abortive "doodles" I made before I could work out how best to deploy my range of yarns to suggest the luxurious, undulating, overlapping vegetation.

I continued working throughout in double crochet using a large hook but, after the first 14 rows and on the right side of the fabric only, I began to work long trebles, mostly quadruple, quintuple and sextuple, round the stem of a stitch several rows below, but always together with double crochet on the current row so that the fabric remained consistently stable. The long trebles were worked slanting either to the left or right of the perpendicular, never straight up and down, for the plant must curve from its first emergence from the water. There are no straight lines in nature!

After another 4 rows I began working some long trebles round previous long trebles as well as round the stitches in the main fabric a few rows below. By working long trebles round long trebles I could continue or change the colour, and at the same time continue or change the direction of the curve of the now elongated plant growing up from the pond or emerging from the undergrowth, remembering that with every curve and bend the leaf blade would present a different angle to the light and change colour accordingly, perhaps from dark green to turquoise, to malachite, to emerald, to viridian green. Each leaf would be different, here and there shaded by its neighbours, here and there exposed to full sunlight, and among the tall leaves or at the head of a flower-stem I worked long trebles in amethyst, lavender, or deep purple-blue mohair to suggest the irises. The flowers were distributed rather sparsely, hints rather than statements.

Garment Design

The design of the garment was, of necessity, kept very simple. The only seams were at the shoulders.

I worked throughout to a tension of approximately 12sts and 14 rows double crochet to 10cm (4") square.

I began on a foundation chain of 102sts with 1ch to turn on each row. After working eight rows straight I placed a safety-pin marker in the 26th and 77th stitch of the row, to determine the positions of the side underarm shaping. Required increases were carried out on either side of the marker pin at evenly spaced intervals as the work progressed until the long band measured 25-26cm (10") from the base and fitted me comfortably (loosely rather than tightly) when I wrapped it round me under the arms, the edges of the band meeting at centre front.

The pin was moved to the stitch immediately above as every new row was worked. Work was then continued on the back and on each front section separately.

The first row of the back section was worked over the fifty stitches between the marker pins, and the first row of each front section of the 25sts before and after the marker pin. The marked stitch was left unworked at the base of the armhole.

Shaping for arm-holes, front edges and back neck were worked as appropriate. After joining the shoulders, a border was worked in double crochet round fronts and back neck, using two strands of different shades of green in 4-ply wool, and changing one colour of the pair on every row exactly as for the waist band. This time the slubbed yarn was omitted. Hook size was changed when necessary to produce the tension required. I used only three rows double crochet and 1 row crab stitch for a border 2cm (3/4") wide. 4 buttonholes were spaced at regular intervals on the straight edge of the right front border (left as you look at it from the front) and 4 buttons were crocheted to fit. For these only one strand of 4-ply was used with a 2.50mm hook.

Armhole borders were worked in the same way, but with 2 instead of 3 rows double crochet before the crab stitch finish.

CHAPTER SIX

"ROUEN CATHEDRAL, Harmonie brune" - after Monet

"Rouen Cathedral" like "Irises" was based on a reproduction of a Monet painting but it is a much earlier piece of work. I had seen the original painting, together with the other Cathedrals, many years before I had ever given so much as a thought to crochet - a craft with which I was quite unfamiliar.

I came across this particular reproduction in a book, entitled "Harmonie brune" at a time when I was becoming excited about textiles and beginning to find my way about crochet. I was already feeling adventurous enough to improvise on techniques already learned, sometimes in order to solve a problem, sometimes simply to see what happened.

Day after day I was discovering new and different ways of enriching and developing a texture and, coming across "Harmonie brune" and observing Monet's rendering of the cathedral's great mass, scale, solidity and strength so emphatically, while at the same time portraying with equal emphasis, the almost lace-like delicacy of its ornament and conjuring the illusion of lightness (in contrast to the great weight below) as the building soared up towards the sky. I was enchanted.

The longer and more carefully I studied the small reproduction the more strongly I was tempted to respond with a "commentary" in crochet.

The reproduction does not and cannot show the trembling modulations of light which you see in the original painting nor the subtle vibrancy which makes stillness more still and quietness more quiet, like the trills at the end of Beethoven's Sonata Opus 111. These unearthly heights of art are way beyond the limits of craftsmanship, but there was, nevertheless, a treasure-trove to be discovered and enjoyed in a different, if more modest way, in what the little reproduction had to offer.

It seemed feasible to work section by section, a rectangle of a size which could, when folded round the body with the two side edges meeting at the front and with spaces left unworked from the position between under arm and shoulder through which the arms could pass, become a full length sleeveless coat fastened by buttons at the shoulders. Alternatively when spread out to full width and suspended from a rod, it could become a wall-hanging showing the whole twilit front of the cathedral.

Once the full length required for the coat was decided the size of the complete rectangle could be determined. Almost no modifications of Monet's picture were needed. The view of the cathedral had been painted directly from the front. All the sections were plotted to scale on graph paper incorporating the armhole slits in the spaces between the towers. But there is a long way to go between the visualisation of the design and its realisation.

Selecting yarns

Finding all the yarns for "Harmonie Brune" was difficult and time consuming. So many shades of brown and grey were needed and so many textures, each one of which would reflect the light differently. I could not predict what quantity I would need of any yarn used and I found I needed many more yarns than I had anticipated. I had to consider the thickness, the weight and the "feel" of every yarn, discover how it would handle and whether it would or would not combine well with other yarns selected. I searched the resources of specialist suppliers (some of which operated a mail-order service which proved helpful) as well as mills and wool-shops and, when all the range of yarns was collected together, there was the problem of finding storage space at home. Living with crochet is not always easy!

I began my cathedral by working the three doors and their respective tympana then proceeding to build up the decorative arches framing them. I always worked on the right side of the fabric and raised each arch from the innermost to the outermost of the range of successive arches in progressively higher relief to indicate the gradual recession leading back inwards to the deep set doorway and, at the same time, varying the type of stitch used and the shades of brown and grey to maintain a rich texture suggesting the changes of light and shade on and within the curves of the arches.

In the upper sections of the work I made much more use of lighter shades of colour and lighter weights of yarn and, by means of surface crochet I attempted to represent the delicate traceries which, as the building rose up higher and higher, appeared as frail - seeming as cobwebs as more and more of the pearly evening light reached them.

It was while striving to achieve this etherial effect that I made a very near fatal blunder. However, as each completed section was placed in position on a sheet spread on the floor and joined, my cathedral still looked splendid. Very few finishing touches were required. Agates were attached to the front ties and an inconspicuous corded edge worked on the front edges.

Agates were chosen because their colours corresponded to the greys and browns used in the fabric.

Finally I worked a dense row of fine, pale grey boucle yarn to represent the parapets on the upper ledges and, concealed within them, buttons and buttonholes to fasten at the shoulders when the cathedral was used as a coat. All that remained now was to see whether my idea worked.

I fastened the buttons at the shoulders and tried on the coat, then turned to view it from every angle in the looking-glass.

It was then that disaster struck! No - the mirror did not crack from side to side like the Lady of Shalott's but for a moment at least I felt every bit as doom-stricken as that poor lady.

What had happened? The weight of yarn in the heavy main doorway and its surrounding arches caused the fabric to jut out at a preposterous angle just over my bottom. My cathedral, which had looked so beautiful when laid out flat on the floor, was a ruin! Worse still - a ridiculous ruin!

At this point I seem to remember my husband gave me a large neat whisky! I have no very clear recollections. But a few minutes later, when the first shock was over, I picked up the phone and succeeded in making immediate contact with Pauline Turner in Lancaster. What it is to have friends, especially friends who can perform miracles!

Pauline left everything she was doing, jumped into her car (with a supply of firm iron-on cotton lining) and was with me in Alderley Edge, Cheshire, an hour later. Within minutes of her arrival the lining had been securely fixed in place and its edges trimmed all ready to be turned in and stitched down. This magnificent rescue service, which I shall ever remember with gratitude, effected a complete cure.

Fourteen years later "Rouen Cathedral" still hangs well both as a coat and as a wall hanging.

I learned a very important lesson from this mistake. When constructing a piece of work in which many different weights of yarn are combined, the weight must be distributed evenly. In this instance, with the help of Pauline's resourcefulness, it was possible to overcome the problem by using a lining, but I would always prefer to use crochet unlined to avoid any undesirable rigidity. With intelligent planning (and much more sense than I used here) crochet can almost always be planned so that it holds its shape without any tendency to bulge or sag even after years of use. I learned my lesson the hard way!

CHAPTER SEVEN

"MOSSY WALL"

The original mossy wall ran beside a narrow strip of garden outside one of the windows of our ground floor apartment in a farmhouse near the Trough of Bowland where we spent a short holiday.

I had spent the previous five days at Pauline Turner's Crochet Course in Morecambe working with my teachers, James Walters, Sylvia Cosh and Pauline herself, and when I came away my eyes were still seeing everything I looked at in terms of crochet. When I sat by that window facing the low stone wall, covered with lichens and cushions of moss, I saw it all in crochet.

Since we had come directly from Morecambe I had with me my collection of hooks and a car loaded with boxes and bulging bags containing the vast array of yarns with which I had experimented during the Crochet Course. I only had to rummage among them to find all I needed to begin to "doodle" as I sat by the window and looked at the wall in the different light of early morning, late afternoon and early evening.

Most of each day we spent walking in that beautiful country-side, with a break for a pub-lunch, of course. It was still early July and the weather was perfect, sunny from dawn till dusk. The wild-roses were in full bloom in the lanes, and the grassy verges bright with blue speedwell, starwort and wild orchids - like a medieval tapestry. The woods were cool and moist, and by the streams the liverworts glistened. By tea-time each day I was happy to sit and rest - not by the large window looking out over the harvest fields and the whale-back hills, but at the little window through which I could look at the mossy wall warmed by the sunlight that now, towards the end of the day, touched it with almost level rays and picked out, with pre-Raphaelite precision, every detail of colour and texture. The sun shone through the tiny leaves of the moss, the solid green became translucent, gold and tinged with pink. The brown stalks of the spore bearing capsules became scarlet or purple. The compressed colonies of lichens which, during the day, lay flat against the wall in dull orange patches glowed and glimmered as the evening light reached into the scalloped rosettes, exploring the layers and lifting them, exposing the convexities of their slightly swollen lobes, embroidering them with bright gold and warming the browns and silvering the greys.

I did not, of course, attempt to represent any of this detail naturalistically but I thought my yarns could be combined and related in ways that would express something of the sheer delight I felt in looking at the weathered old wall and perhaps keep something of its memory.

I constructed a stable background of raised trebles, sometimes raising the trebles on the wrong side of the fabric only, sometimes only on the right side, providing surfaces for varying the spacing of the yarns and the type of surface crochet suggested to me by the particular character of each individual yarn and the part it could play, or could be coaxed to play, in this evocation of the mossy wall right there before me. I had, for example, a marvellous Bernat Klein yarn in which at least four different shades of green and brown were irregularly combined in different thicknesses and textures, ranging from a fine silky thread to full-bodied, bulky knops of almost unspun yarn in which all the colours opened up and were displayed in larger areas but always in subtly different blending. I worked the lengths of the finely spun sections, where the colours were more densely concentrated, in very small chain stitches on the smooth surface of the main fabric, then allowed the bulky sections, which tapered at each end of its length, to come into "full bloom" and display its colours in one very large chain. I repeated the sequences of large and small chains at irregular intervals in accordance with the yarn. An extraordinary yarn such as this makes the impossible, possible; you simply have to let it speak for itself.

Since the design for the "Mossy Wall" waistcoat developed directly from the initial "doodling" I have shown its detailed construction in the diagram on page 16. I do not, of course, suggest that it should or could be exactly copied because few of the yarns I used are still available, but it is possible that the method of approach could be helpful.

I had learned from my cathedral coat/wall-hanging project how important it is, when working with many different yarns - firm ones, flimsy ones, light-weight and heavy ones, to think most carefully how they would best work together, not only to express my ideas most clearly and imaginatively, but to produce a stable, well-balanced design which will hold its shape - and preserve those first, exciting ideas - over the years.

It is very rarely that "inspiration" for crochet - the intense visual and tactile delight that demands, irresistibly, some active response - can be realised while the source of that inspiration is still in front of your eyes. "Snowflakes in Summer" and "Mossy Wall" were lucky exceptions. It is rare, too, that "inspiration" is quite so simple and direct.

The thoughts and feelings which contribute to most projects I have attempted are far-reaching and complex. There is, of course, the immediacy of my response to certain yarns and to virtually anything which stimulates and pleases my eyes and sense of touch, especially when I am taken suddenly by surprise, and I see and feel with unusual concentration as so often happens when I am on holiday or in unfamiliar surroundings. These periods of heightened attention, however brief, bring back the sense of seeing the world new again, luminous, and with extraordinary clarity as if seeing it for the very first time as in early childhood and, with the recovery of this "visionary gleam", the immediate object of attention is seen through many transparent layers of memory and association. "Marguerites" and "Summer Meadow", inspired by the lovely yarns I saw and touched, reach back through the years. I followed, quite literally, the threads which led me back into childhood and restored to me whole constellations of happy memories. But which really came first, the yarns or the memories? They are inextricably interwoven. The child deep in the meadow grasses and lost to sight was - is - still very much alive, though most of the time asleep. The touch of the yarns woke her like a Prince's kiss woke the Sleeping Beauty. Perhaps

we should pause from time to time and ask ourselves why we should choose to crochet rather than to paint. I do not think it is because it is easier to crochet than to paint. Painting, in fact, comes naturally to almost every child, and crochet, once it becomes adventurous, makes enormous demands on ingenuity and technical resources - there is no end to the problem-solving. I suspect that crochet, which like painting, can open up new worlds of colour can, at the same time, allows us to explore a world of touch, marvellously subtle and satisfying, and is the secret of its special appeal.

Working notes for
"Mossy Wall" Waistcoat

Vertical panels for surface crochet are worked with a DK yarn and 4.50mm hook or hook size to produce tension of 12sts to 9cm (3.5").

Panels and borders are worked mainly in 4 ply yarns with 3.50mm hook in dc and ch, to produce the tension 4 patt rep (4 grs) to 11cm (4.5").

Dc and ch pattern [in 4-ply]   Worked over a multiple of 3+1 sts (3+2ch) in 4 ply with 3.50mm hook.

Tension sample: 14ch, 1dc 1ch 1dc in 2nd ch from hook, *2ch, miss 2ch, 1dc 1ch 1dc in next ch [1 Vst made], rep from * to end.

Next and every following row: 1Vst in first Vst, *2ch, miss 2ch, 1Vst in next Vst, rep from * to end, 1ch, turn. Each repeat = 1 patt gr.

Dch and ch pattern [in DK]

To change this patt from a 4 ply to a DK yarn use 4.00mm or 4.50mm hook to maintain tension (check as work proceeds).First row: 1ch, turn, 2dc in first Vst, *1ch, turn, miss 2ch, 2dc [1Vst made] in next Vst, rep from * to end.

Longer Jacket (fringe optional)

Work extra ch in foundation ch when beginning work (centre back panel) but always in multiples of 3 to accommodate dc and ch patt as used in this design.

Snowflakes in Summer

Owl and Flower
Coat (front and back)

Plate 2

Summer Meadow

Marguerites

Plate 3

Kathleen Basford's
Irises

The original postcard
of Monet's Irises

Plate 4

Rouen Cathedral: Harmonie brune
(after Monet)

Mossy Wall
The Changing Light

Morning

Evening

Plate 6

Liverworts
and Mosses

Plate 7

Fast Train to Fritzler (front and back)

Plate 8

Lichens
(front and back)

Larches and Lichens

note: length of waistcoat = 45cm (approx 18") plus 9cm (3 1/2") fringe = 54cm but if a longer length waistcoat is preferred work 12 more sts on starting chain (foundation) chain and on every row.

12sts = 9cm using DK with 4.50mm hook.

Waistcoat is joined at sides and shoulders.

Border is worked all round Fronts and Back neck after joining sides and shoulders. 3 rows dc and ch patt, beginning at Right Front, lower corner, making 4 button holes on first row for larger "mossy" buttons. (See notes for small buttonholes if preferred).

1 row dc and ch patt border round each armhole.

Buttonholes

For large fancy buttons work as shown in diagram.

For buttons of 0.5" diameter or less there is no need to work buttonholes at all as small buttons can be pushed through the 2ch spaces.

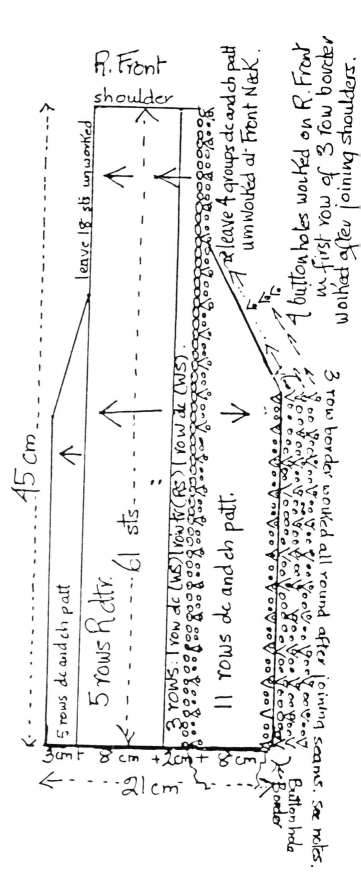

For buttons 1" diameter, work each buttonhole as follows when using a 4ply yarn and 3.50mm hook: 1dc in Vst, 4ch, miss 2ch, 1dc in next Vst.

On the following row work 1Vst into dc, 2ch, miss 4ch, 1Vst in next dc.

Buttonhole row for 1" diameter button

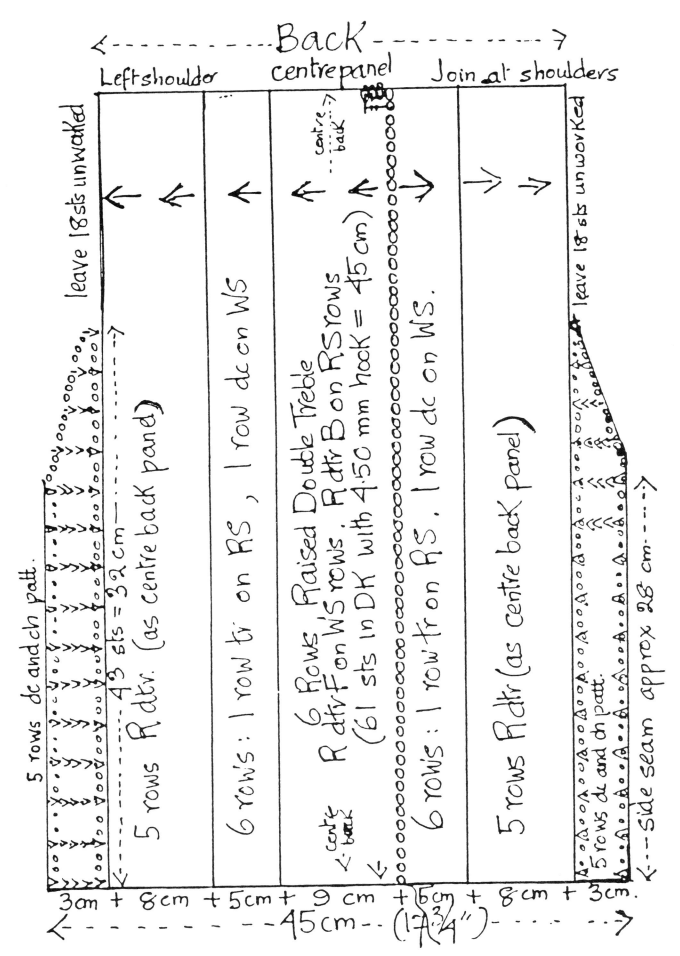

Diagram to show general construction of
"Mossy Wall" Waistcoat

CHAPTER EIGHT

"LIVERWORTS AND MOSSES"

After completing "Mossy Wall" I could say no more about mosses (and there was much left unsaid) until I found a range of Bernat Klein's brushed mohairs in which every natural looking shade of every species of moss appeared, living and vibrant, and all of such mossy softness that you longed to plunge your hands into its delicious depths.

They were like no other mohairs I had ever seen before or have ever seen again. They were dyed after brushing, each with seven or more colours, and they reflected the light in such a way that every nuance of every colour was enhanced. (It was, of course, one of these mohairs that made possible my "Summer Meadow" cape) With the help of these lovely mohairs I could visualise wrapping myself up in mosses, and with this thought came the idea for my "Mosses and Liverworts" jacket.

I thought of the mosses of moorland bogs and the mosses in damp woods where, also, liverworts flourished side by side with them - I wanted them all. I wanted to be surrounded by them and by all the happy associations they evoked, a sweet play-time world reaching deeply into and through every part of my life from infancy to the present day; not always accessible but never wholly irrecoverable.

I wanted the brilliant mosses to float to the surface over a darker background, which could suggest dead leaves, tree bark or leaf mould -whatever, so I combined the Bernat Klein mohairs with an unbrushed mohair of dark mixed greens and browns and a velvety chenille that toned with all the mosses. Used the chenille for the unobtrusive edgings and buttons of the jacket, and also for the pocket linings which, worked with a 6.00mm hook to a tension of 18 rows dc on a base of 14 stitches, measured approximately 20cm long and 14cm wide. This basic tension thus established, was only slightly modified as different yarns were introduced into the main fabric but, as shown in Diagram 2, there was no deviation of sufficient significance to cause distortion.

On right side rows I worked the mohairs in long trebles (each long treble together with one double crochet, to avoid leaving a hole) but always into the main fabric and never, as in "Irises", round long trebles lying below. The technique was used in this project simply as a means of varying the combinations of colours in the Bernat Klein mohairs in as many different ways as possible; no two stitches lying side by side over two, three or four rows were ever alike, the colours down the length of each stitch always changing, and no combination of colours ever exactly repeated. Since my object was to create a moss garden I did not want individual stitches to stand out too conspicuously but rather that they should appear to advance out of, or recede into, the background at irregular intervals, gently and softly. I wanted to exploit as fully as I could the potentialities of these lovely yarns and display the brilliance and lustre of their colours, but I also wanted an over-all impression that would not only excite the eyes, but would at the same time, be restful to look at, easy and natural. Of course, my "vision" was not fully realised, but it never is.

After completing the jacket - the "moss-garden" - I began to introduce liver-worts (a perfectly natural association) into the lower parts of the main fabric, but watching most carefully that the extra weight did not pull the upper part of the garment out of shape. I attempted to represent the liverworts more "realistically", choosing *Marchantia polymorpha* for my model because I could not resist the delightful archegonia which stand up on the thallus (the leafy part of the plant) like tiny umbrellas. I dyed 4 ply wool in a range of colours as close as possible to the colours in the mohair but mostly in more subdued shades because I did not want "blobs" of strong colour which could possibly out-shout or in any way diminish the beauty of the mohairs or intrude stridently into the quiet depths of my moss-garden. I have described in detail how I made my liverworts in the section "Surface Crochet".

You can find excellent photographs of Marchantia and other liverworts as well as photographs, all of them equally good, of every kind of moss and lichen in Roger Phillips' book "Grasses, Ferns, Mosses and Lichens of Great Britain and Ireland" published in large format paper-back by Pan Books Ltd in 1980 and still, happily, in print. I have found this a most useful work of reference and full of ideas for crochet. It was from photographs shown on pages 182 and 183 of this book that I found the primary source of inspiration for my next project, "Lichens".

CHAPTER NINE

"LICHENS"

The idea for this particular enterprise - a play on the theme of lichens - first came from photographs, as already mentioned; but I doubt if I would have responded so strongly to the photographs had I never actually observed and handled specimens of the living plants. Close inspection, under magnification, reveals fascinating details of their structure, of their texture and of their surprising colours that would never be noticed and certainly never appreciated by a cursory glance. It is only in country areas, where the air is clean and free from pollution that you can hope to find a rich variety of lichens, but they are worth searching for. They are among the most beautiful, strange and interesting of living organisms.

The photographs in Roger Phillips' book were not only inspiring but also very helpful when I was searching for yarns. Even though I was always thinking about lichens in three dimensions I could use the photographs to see the colours in two dimensions which somewhat simplified the problem.

I found a boucle yarn of a bluish-grey colour that corresponded almost exactly with the colour and all the light and dark shadings of *Hypogymnia physodes* (shown on Pg.178 of Phillips' book) and which I could work, using a 6.00mm hook, to exactly the same tension as that of the "Mosses and Liverworts" design. I made the whole jacket with this yarn, aiming to produce a stable mesh of double crochet, light-weight over all but firm enough to carry the weight of all the yarns I chose for the three dimensional lichens which I proposed to elaborate in surface crochet. I bought more of this ground-base yarn than I needed for the jacket since I knew that I would require an ample supply to work the foundation of all the experimental samples I might require for trying out every other yarn that could contribute to the development of the forms and textures of the different lichens and see how I could bring them together in the most natural-looking relationships.

I made my first experimental samples trying to re-create the species of Cladonia shown on pages 182 and 183 of Roger Phillip's book because it was such fun trying to improvise the scarlet-tipped spore-bearing structures (see section "Surface Crochet").

However, while working on a series of "doodles" I realised I would need a more extensive range of yarns than I had anticipated. I could find the desired textures (an unbrushed mohair with tiny loops and a silky sheen, and a fine chenille proved particularly useful) but not in the full range of closely related colours necessary to represent adequately the very subtle changes of colour found in lichens, so, once again, Granny spent many more hours dyeing in the kitchen! And once again it happened, so appropriately, that Helena modelled the finished project.

I spent much time and effort on the experimental swatches (my "doodles"). I laid them flat on the floor so that I could stand up and look down on them (a "bird's eye" view) and I placed them on a neutral background in a vertical position and looked at them from the other side of the room. Many samples were discarded at this stage. Then I tried arranging and re-arranging the surviving samples until I could relate one to another in a way that began to suggest something near to natural organic growth. I wanted an arrangement that looked inevitable, the only arrangement possible.

The whole must always add up to more than the sum of the parts, and it was particularly important to me that I should achieve an over-all sense of harmony when trying to say something about lichens. I wanted the whole to express my very special feeling for lichens, each of which consists of two quite different but mutually dependent life-forms - a fungus and an alga. The fungus draws moisture and minerals from the substance on which the plant grows, and the chloroplasts in the alga converts them into nutrients. Every lichen is a perfectly balanced working partnership between two entirely different organisms. I like this.

CHAPTER TEN

"FAST TRAIN TO FRITZLAR"

I did not begin work on the project I called "Fast Train to Fritzlar" until some four or five years after making the journey it commemorated. At that time crochet played no part at all in my life. I had no idea whatsoever of its potentialities. If ever I thought about it at all, it was something I associated with antimacassars, doilies and dreary gentility; I never had any inclination to learn how to do it. I had no interest in any hobbies or pastimes. I never had any spare time to "pass". My life was fully occupied with my work some of which, happily, spilled over into interests I shared with my family and friends. Very occasionally I knitted for my grandchildren and because of this I watched the BBC series "Knitting Fashion" (1977 or thereabouts) and for the first time saw James Walters. For the first time too, I saw crochet -it hit me with enormous impact! I wrote at once to James who linked me up with Pauline Turner and that opened up another world to me. This crochet was not a "hobby" - something peripheral to serious concerns. Crochet was a serious concern. I saw it as a means of expressing poetry and passion, and of exploring beyond the immediate experience and reaching deeply into memory and recovering moments - hours - of intense excitement and pleasure - such as I have already described in connection with "Summer Meadow" and "Marguerites", and such as I felt on the morning I travelled by high-speed train to Fritzlar.

I was going to Fritzlar to photograph some carvings in the cathedral there, and the railway track passed through many miles of unspoiled virgin forest. It was October, and the trees in the forest and the bracken growing on the narrow verges on either side of the track had changed from summer into full autumn colouring, and the dazzling sunlight and speed of the train blurred these colours in ever-changing kaleidoscopic patterns. We stood by the window and watched; watched and wondered.

It is an awe-inspiring experience to be enclosed in deep forest. We were confronted by a vast, silent mystery, stretching, not only over many miles of what was then West Germany, but stretching back through time, through history, through and beyond and before man-made divisions between one country and another, before the first naming of countries and the fixing of boundaries - names and boundaries that have changed many times during the course of the movements, peaceful or aggressive, and of the wanderings and wars of different occupying or invading human populations, long before roads and railway tracks running through Germany and other European countries had such horrific associations. The forest pre-dates all human nightmares and stands today pure and uncontaminated.

It was not only the visual beauty of the ever-changing yet never-changing scenery through which we were passing so swiftly that moved me so deeply, it was the sense of continuity. Nature builds 'cathedrals' more majestic and more beautiful than any built by man. Man-made buildings decay and fall into ruins, like all artifacts, but natural forest is self-renewing. Its only serious predator and parasite is man.

The memory of that journey to Fritzlar is imprinted indelibly in my mind and, in later years, I wanted to try to express, however inadequately, something of its meaning for me.

Recalling the sumptuous colours and the play of light upon them, I began to collect small quantities of each and every yarn I could find which matched my memory. I chose a brushed DK yarn, "random" dyed in shades of yellow, orange and russet with which to construct the basic fabric and ground plan for a waistcoat. This yarn would only be seen on the inside of the finished garment where it would serve as a smooth, neat "lining". The design was worked in raised treble raising the stitches on every row but so that the ridges lay on the right side of the fabric only, running from the top of the waist at the front, over the shoulder, to the top of the waist at the back.

Each ridge was overworked in surface crochet, using whatever technique best suited the thickness and texture of the yarn selected. Only short lengths along the ridge were worked in any colour, I changed the colour and, often texture of the yarn at irregular intervals, and always leaving the last stitch of the section on a safety-pin. The idea of leaving the last stitch "on hold" was to make it quite easy to remove and change any section that did not, on review, blend perfectly into the whole scheme or accord agreeably with all of its near or remote neighbours. At the end of each day I would place the work on a neutral background in a vertical position on the far side of the room, and look at it again with fresh eyes the following morning. I would replace any inharmonious sections, but again leave the replacement "on hold". Not until the whole work was finished were the pins removed and the sections secured into place.

So slowly did this work proceed! I spent many more hours pulling yarns out than putting them in - so many adjustments and modulations were necessary. I wanted to suggest how the tree trunks looked as we flashed by them - how they disappeared into the heavy canopy of foliage falling down from high above to ground level. As the foliage descended the colours appeared darker and richer. The colours up above were more closely blended, less distinct one from another as more and more light reached them until they seemed to dissolve in light. It was, in fact very simple work, but the colour revision, the different placements and replacements necessary before the relationships, the light and shade, began to look more like what I remembered seeing, required great patience and much more time.

After the main fabric was finished and the seams joined I worked a band of raised treble ribbing into the edge stitches all round the waist, trying to suggest the rich tangle of bright bracken and weeds, variously brown, gold, and green, at the edge of the forest, and I worked narrow - almost invisible - edgings and buttons correspondingly.

I wanted very much to express, as well as I could, my intense enjoyment of what had seemed like a long-extended fire-work display of colour, exploding and falling down in fountains of splendour, and all so silently; but what I wanted, even more, was to express my awareness of the contrast between the timelessness of the forest, its continuity and survival, and my own rapid passage through it - so transitory - gone in a flash!

(See Chapter 12: Foundation Shape for instructions [p 24] and diagram [p25]

CHAPTER ELEVEN

"LARCH AND LICHENS"

Like "Irises", "Larch and Lichens" began with a gift - not a post-card this time, but a branch from a larch tree, with clusters and tufts of lichen on it. It had been cut from a tree growing near James Walter's country home in Wales. It was presented to me by James and Sylvia - perhaps as another crochet challenge - and how could I resist? - but primarily because they knew how much pleasure it would give me. We have shared so many joys together in the years since our first meeting in 1978.

I looked long and hard at the lichen-laden branch and started to see it as crochet, and not the branch only; I could visualise the tree from which it came - and the surrounding trees, all draped with lichen, and I could visualise, furthermore, a finished garment which seemed to emanate from a misty Welsh landscape - its gentle air, its gentle conifers and lovely lichens - all crochet.

Most coniferous trees produce their branches in irregular whorls, growth patterns which allow the light to reach all the needles as the branches spread wide, never quite over-lapping the layer below. The branches of larch tend to spread in upward - sweeping curves - a feature more clearly seen in winter because, unlike other conifers, larches are deciduous.

I chose a very soft, misty yarn of rather indefinite grey - putty shadings - with a hint of yellow here - a hint of blue there. With this yarn I made the foundation of a simple sleeveless jacket with no seams other than those at the shoulder - I worked it in a curving wave pattern, raising the stitches on both sides of the fabric so that the inside of the garment also rippled in well defined waves. I did not want a straight line anywhere.

I chose a rough textured raw silk, about DDK thickness, and brown-speckled, rather similar to the branches of pine. I let the branches curve across the wave-pattern of the foundation and sometimes follow the curves and then covered them with lichens.

I had a rich-treasure hoard of yarns to play with. From time to time I bought yarns - usually quite small quantities - simply because they reminded me of things I liked - usually a plant or part of a plant. How pleasant it was to rummage through this collection and find yarns that had made me think of silver-weed growing by the road-side, or pussy willow in early spring; woolly catkins and silver, fluttering leaves of aspens; or cotton-grass growing on the moors; quaking-grass; hair's-tail grass; thistle-down and dandelion clocks, and robin's pincushions growing on wild rose leaves parasitised by gall-wasps - and a yarn that had looked like the hairy seeds of travellers joy, untidy and straggling over hedges in autumn. As I sorted through them I discovered changes of association - the yarns were already transforming into lichens. I did not try to represent particular lichens as I had tried with Cladonia, though one of them, trailing in long fringes, looked remarkably like a species of *Usnea* (Phillips.*loc sit*. P.186) but I do not know if it ever grows on larch in Wales.

I enjoyed making this one because I combined two yarns - a green one to represent the algal element and a light, knoppy one to represent the fungus. But, having chosen my yarns I let my fancy stray freely. My imagination luxuriated in lichens.

The only motif I tried to represent more or less naturalistically was the larch one. This was a simple modification of the "curlicue". (See James Walter's "New Crochet Workshop", 1992, Part 5) . Using a fine brown yarn with a small hook - 2.00mm - I made a short length of chain then worked about five trebles in the third chain from the hook and into every following chain to the end. This coiled round itself in a tight firm spiral, producing an excellent larch cone! - and, I could use them very effectively as buttons. I scattered my larch cones generously on the branches letting them nestle among the various lichens.

Of all my ideas, I think "Larch and Lichens" was the one that worked most successfully. Although it tended more to 'abstraction' than to 'realism' I thought when Helena stood looking through the branches of a pine tree in our garden to model it, it fitted quite naturally in this setting.

I came to regard the branch given to me by Sylvia and James as a magic wand. I kept it long after the jacket was finished but sadly, the lichens succumbed to the effects of our central heating and polluted air, shrivelled and fell off. I no longer have the branch but I think the magic stayed with me.

CHAPTER TWELVE

FOUNDATION SHAPE

There is no one shape or fabric on which to work surface crochet but there are advantages to using a particular stitch pattern which holds surface crochet firmly whilst still retaining its softness. It is equally important that the weight of the additional material does not distort the shape. One effective base fabric is that of raised trebles and the pattern for a sleeveless jacket using this stitch is given below. Chapter 14 gives additional information on the suitability of stitches when making a crochet base.

There are many excellent reference books on basic stitch techniques and how to work the actual stitches [see pg000]. Everything described here can be achieved using the "Technique of Crochet" written by Pauline Turner and published by Batsford. A long-line jacket using a raised double treble is given on page 97 which can be used as a base for other experimentations.

Instructions given are for bust size 86cm (34") but the design is easily adapted for greater or lesser width or length.

SLEEVELESS TOP IN RAISED TREBLE FOR SURFACE CROCHET

Materials: 5 x 40g balls Georges Picaud Mohair No 1 or Sofil Mohair

2 x 50g balls DK for edgings (welt, button/button-hole border and buttons)

Hook size suggested for DK, 4.50mm for edgings, 2.50mm for buttons.

Hook size suggested for mohair, 6.00mm for base chain, 5.50mm for main part, to produce the tension suggested.

Tension: 14sts = 11cm

11 rows raised treble (Rtr) = 12cm

4.50mm hook used for DK or to produce tension 12sts = 9cm (measured over dc)

Pattern: Right side RS rows - 2ch, turn, RtrB to last st, 1tr in last st.

Wrong side WS rows - 2ch, turn, RtrF to last st, 1tr in last st.

Left Side Section

With 6.00mm hook make 114ch,

Row 1: change to 5.50mm hook, 1tr in 4th ch from hook, tr to end, 2ch, turn [112sts].

Row 2: With WS facing miss first st (turning ch counts as st) 110RtrF, 1tr in last st, 2ch, turn.

Row 3: With RS facing miss first st, RtrB to last st, 1tr, 2ch, turn.

Continue on 112sts, working RtrF in WS rows and RtrB in RS rows, until 10 rows have been completed, 2ch to turn.

Row 11: 51RtrB, RtrB2tog, 2ch,turn (53sts)

Row 12: RtrF2tog, RtrF to last st, 1tr, 2ch, turn (52sts).

Work 6 more rows straight on 52sts, ending with WS row. Finish off.

With RS facing miss next 10sts of the 58sts left unworked on long panel, join yarn in next st, 3ch, RtrB2tog, RtrB to end, 1tr, 2ch, turn,(46sts) [= row 11]

Next row:[= Row 12], 41RtrF, Rtr2tog, 1tr, 3ch, turn, (44sts)

Next row: [= Row 13], miss first 2sts, RtrB2tog, RtrB to end, 1tr, 2ch, turn.

Continue to decrease 2sts at neck slope edge on every row until 32sts remain. Finish off. [18 rows]

Turn to RS. Rejoin yarn at lower front edge 2ch and working under foundation chain work 35RtrB, RtrB2tog, 3ch, turn.

Next row: miss first st, RtrF2tog, RtrF to end, 1tr, 2ch turn, [36sts].

Work straight in pattern for two more rows. For increased width, decrease one st at armhole curve on 3rd row and complete with 2 or 3 extra rows straight at underarm. (1 row Rtr = approximately 1cm. 1 extra row will add 4cm all round at bust).

Miss next 36sts of long panel for the armhole, join yarn in next st, 3ch, RtrB2tog, Rtr to last st, 1tr, 1ch, turn, [37sts].

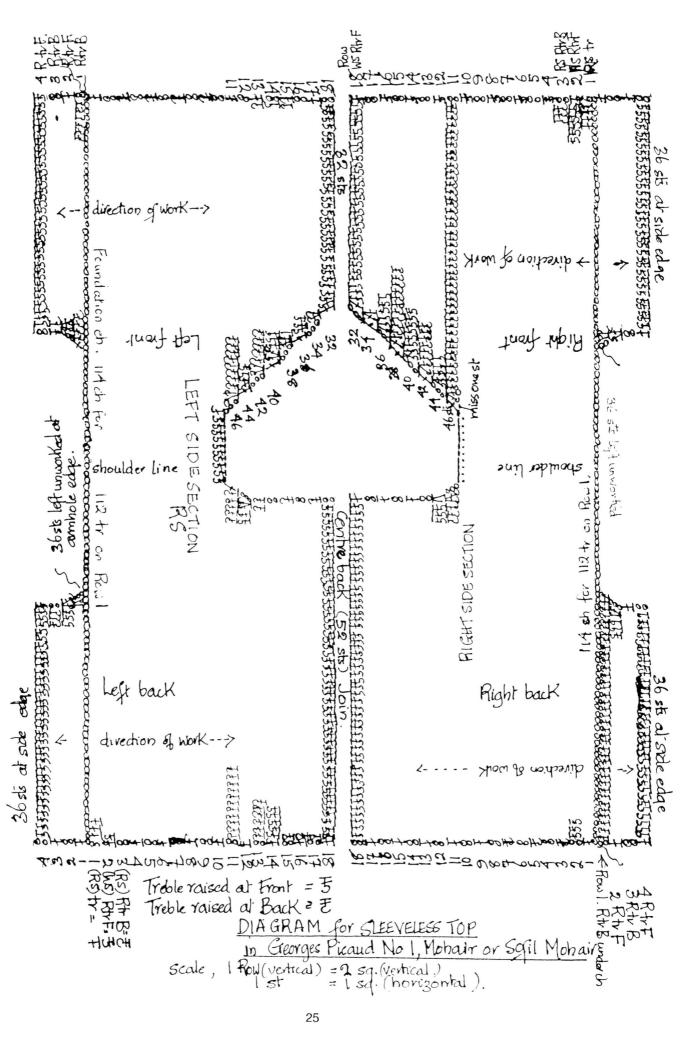

DIAGRAM for SLEEVELESS TOP
in Georges Picaud No 1, Mohair or Sqil Mohair

Treble raised at Front = F
Treble raised at Back = F

Scale , 1 Row (vertical) = 2 sq. (vertical.)
1 st = 1 sq. (horizontal.)

Next row: 34RtrF, Rtr2tog, 2ch, turn [36sts]

Work 2 more rows in patt on these 36sts. [For increased width work 3 instead of 2 decrease rows, and 3 rows straight on 35sts. Note: extra sts will be required for armhole-edgings to correspond.]

Right Side Section

(mirror image of Left Side Section)

Work 10 rows as for Left Side Section.

Row 11: With RS facing 2ch, turn, miss first st, 43RtrB, RtrB2tog, miss next st, 1tr. (2sts decreased) 3ch, turn [46sts].

Row 12: miss first and next st, RtrF2tog, RtrF to last st, 1tr, (2sts decreased) [44sts].

Work 6 more rows decreasing 2sts at front neck slope on every row. 32sts remain. Fasten off.

With RS facing miss next 10sts of long panel. Rejoin yarn in next st, 3ch, miss first st, RtrB2tog, RtrB to end, 1tr, 2ch, turn, (1st decreased) [53sts].

Next row: [= Row 12] RtrF to last 2sts, RtrF2tog, 2ch, turn, [52sts].

Work 6 more rows straight on 52sts. Finish off.

With RS facing join yarn in first st of foundation ch at lower right back, 2ch, 35RtrB worked under ch of tr row, RtrB2tog, 2ch, turn. [37sts]

Next row: RtrF to last 2sts, RtrF2tog, ch2 to turn.

Work 2 more rows straight on 36sts. [Adapt here for larger sizes, see above]. Finish off.

Join at centre back so that the "ridges" formed by the ch tops of sts on last tr row are raised on RS.

Fold over at shoulders and join at sides as at centre back.

For welt, button/button-hole border and armhole edgings use DK with hook size 4.50mm (or to produce tension: 12sts = 9cm measured over dc).

Welt

In raised treble ribbing and with RS facing join yarn in first row end at lower left front (= Row 18) 3ch, *1RtrF under the "ridge" formed by raised sts, 1tr under next row end ("valley"), rep from * to end, 2ch, turn. [176sts].

Next row: *1RtrF in tr, 1RtrB in Rtr under ridges to preserve the continuity of the "ridges" on RS. Work 5 more rows in rib.

Button/button-hole border

With RS facing join yarn to lower right front, 1ch (do not count as st), 8dc in welt, 32dc up front edge, 2dc at corner at beg on neck slope, 2dc in each of the next 8 row ends, dc in each of 10sts left unworked at neck edge (over shoulder), 2dc in each of the 2 rows to back neck, 12dc at back neck, continue down left front to correspond, 1ch (does not count as st), turn, [156sts].

Row 2: Work in dc inc 1st at the corners at beg of front neck slope and dec 1st at each corner of back neck, 1ch.

Row 3: buttonhole row: 2dc, 2ch, miss 2sts, *7dc, 2ch, miss 2sts, rep from *3 times, cont in dc inc as before at beg of front neck slope and (optional) dec in each corner at back neck.

Row 4: As row 2

Row 5: dc to end, 1ch, do not turn.

Row 6: work all round Button/button-hole border and lower edge of welt in crab st. Finish off.

Armhole Edgings

(adjustment for larger size given in square brackets[])

Join DK at underarm in top of seam, 1ch, 1dc in same place, 1dc in next 4 [6] row ends, 1dc in each of the 36 unworked sts, 1dc in next 4 [6] row ends, ss to first st to join, 1ch, turn, [45(49)sts].

Round 2: 3[5]dc, dc2tog (in corner), 34dc, dc2tog, 3dc, ss to join, 1ch, turn, [43(45)sts].

Round 3: as Round 2, do not turn. [41(43)sts].

Round 4: Work all round in crab st. Finish off.

CHAPTER THIRTEEN

SURFACE CROCHET

The Background Fabric

Surface crochet can be worked on any material through which you can poke a hook but

a. It should be capable of supporting the weight of all the extra yarns you propose to use without pulling out of shape.

b. If you are working on a garment it must not be allowed to become too stiff or too heavy for comfort, neither must it be so flimsy that it will sag.

Double crochet and raised sts (eg raised tr and raised dtr) can provide very satisfactory backgrounds, particularly when worked with fairly light-weight or "bulky" yarns, such as mohair, brushed wool, boucle and certain fancy "knoppy" yarns. A tension of 10sts to 10cm (usually with a 6.00mm hook) for dc with these light but bulky yarns or with 2 strands of 4 ply or a fancy yarn of similar thickness used together can provide a very useful background. The dc fabric will not be stiff or "cardboardy"; it will hold shape well; it can be worked on as "mesh". True mesh, ie 1tr, 2ch, 1tr, 2ch etc, would tend to pull out of shape unless over-worked in regular patterns such as Portuguese crochet. It is more difficult to estimate the size of the finished work when a mesh background is used. The shape should not change at all when using dc.

Many different yarns can be combined in the basic fabric providing the over-all tension can be maintained - yarns can be changed at row ends (every row or alternative row) or anywhere within a row to vary colour and texture.

Some surface work can be carried out at the same time, eg. bobbles, puff sts, "Bee" sts, loop or "fur" sts, all worked on wrong side rows, and "spike" sts and long trebles (triple, quadruple, quintuple or sextuple trebles) which are worked on the right side rows.

To work long treble: Wind the yarn as many times round the hook as required, insert hook into selected position in any stitch of any row below (as though working a stitch raised at the front) complete the long tr up to penultimate stage, (2 loops left on hook), insert hook into next st of current dc row, draw loop through, yoh and draw through all loops on hook. You have worked a long tr and dc together. This is to avoid leaving a hole. If you are to work a treble or half treble row, work the long st tog with tr or htr as appropriate.

Fancy yarns, particularly slub yarns with very thick and very thin sections, can be woven into fabric as you go along, working dc over the thread (thin sections or as required) for 3 or 4 sts, then leaving the most fancy part of the yarn at front while you work dc in row as normal, just behind it, for several sts. It is usually better to avoid very long lengths of yarn on the surface between over-worked stitches, they tend to catch and pull out into long loops. It is possible to work on both RS and WS rows, whilst keeping yarn at front on RS.

It goes without saying that the success of surface crochet depends very largely on your choice of yarns. You often require very small quantities so never throw away any "left overs" that might some day be useful. Light coloured left over yarns, including random-dyed yarns can often be re-dyed to suit your project - this can be very well worthwhile. The Russell Method is excellent.

Motifs

The idea is to invent your own! Try everything out first on your sample of background fabric, which becomes your tension sample, called henceforth your "doodle". This is where all the real work is done.

The following examples are only a few of the possibilities. The scope for imaginative development is almost infinite.

Many of my ideas come from mosses and lichens and liverworts as well as from flowers and grasses.

Mosses can be suggested by unbrushed "loopy" mohair, dyed to suitable colour(s) and worked in "fur" st - using a 4.00mm or 3.50mm hook. You find as you experiment that you will select your hook to suit your yarn and your stitch just as a painter will select a brush for a particular bit of work.

Leaf shapes (eg. oak type leaf) can be made from short lengths of braid. Make 4ch and into 4th ch from hook work 1 trtr and 1dc, *3ch, turn, 1trtr 1dc in dc of previous row, rep from * as many times as you wish then work in surface ss down "mid-rib", continue for 3 or 4 more ch, turn and ss in each ch, for stalk. Several variations of this braid can be tried, substitute dtr or tr for trtr. These motifs are made separately and sewn in position afterwards.

Lichens

Branched types: try Arch Mesh and Picot Mesh, worked directly on background in chenille, DK and boucle yarns with 3.50mm hook.

"Cup" shapes eg. "*Cladonia*":

Choose 4 ply or DK yarn and use 3.00mm or 2.50mm hook. Work on your dc fabric as though it were a mesh (as for Portuguese crochet as described in Pauline's Technique of Crochet)

Cup-shapes

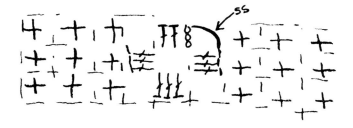

Work 1ch and 11tr all round the 4 sides between 2sts and 2 rows, ss to join. Work some cup-shapes from the inner side and some from the outer side so that the RS and WS of sts are differently featured. Your yarn will determine which is best for your purpose.

The cup shapes can be developed by working in contrasting yarn round outer, inner or both loops of sts. Corals and sea-anemones could be tried. There are all sorts of possibilities in "marine biology" generally.

Lichen cups on stalks: about 6ch, turn and ss in each ch, 1ch and ss up other side of ch again, 3ch, now work 8-10tr in tip of "stalk", ss to top of ch to join in cup-shape. This motif may be worked directly into fabric or made separately and stitched on afterwards.

Match-stalk lichens: make in the same way as open cup lichens but work fewer tr in tip unless very fine yarn is used). Draw up the top of the cup with gathering thread and work a small French Knot in scarlet (or brown) at tip.

Liverworts : eg. *Pellia epiphylla*
Thallus ("leafy" part)

Use a 4 ply green yarn with 3.50mm or 3.00mm hook. Work tr round 3, 2 or occasionally 4 sides of your dc "mesh". This is like Portuguese crochet but worked freely and irregularly so that "folds" and "lobes" are produced in the "thallus" - you may vary the number of tr on each side, sometimes 3tr as in cup shapes, sometimes 5tr to make the thallus fan out, sometimes only 2, to make the folds.

Liverwort (*Marchantia*)
Female plant (*archegonia*)

These umbrella-like structures have 9 spreading rays. Using 4 ply yarn with 2.00, 2.50 or 3.00mm hook as required and yellow/green colours, 7ch, turn, ss in every ch, 1ch, turn, ss up other side of chain, 3ch, work 9 bullion sts in tip of "stalk", ss to top of 3ch to join. Allow the sts to turn back (instead of cup-shape) to form the "umbrella". You may vary the size of these structures and colour so that you have young ones and old ones. Wind yarn about 10 times round 2.00mm hook for each bullion st for small "umbrellas"; 12-15 times round 3.00mm hook for larger ones. Stitch into the "thallus".

Examples which can be worked on or in between the deep "ridges" formed by raised sts.

The basic fabric is usually tr or dtr with each st raised at the front on WS rows and raised at the back on RS rows, so that the "ridges" occur, in fairly close alignment, on the RS of the work only. For wider spacing of the "ridges", eg. in preparation for surface loop st, sts are raised at the front (or the back) on every row so that only alternate rows are raised in "ridges" on RS of the work.

A. Surface crochet - tambour method

This is a surface slip stitch where the supply thread is kept at the back of the work and the hook pushed through the fabric from the front to pick up and pull through the loop for every stitch, rather like the action of a sewing machine (or tambour work in embroidery). A chain is formed on the surface. This can be useful for working in the "valleys" between the "ridges". Tambour chains of various length can be worked, and not necessarily all equal in length. The interest will depend largely on the yarn used because this method does not offer great scope for development, but see the next section surface crochet for further possibilities.

B. Surface crochet - textured

The supply yarn is kept at the front in this and all the following examples.

1. Slip st

Ss in every st of the row of raised sts, working in the normal way under both loops at the head of the st. This row of ss will lie to the side of the "ridge", forming a chain on the near side (as you work) and a single line of "back st" like machine stitching on the far side. This simple technique offers considerable scope for subtle colour blending.

2. Twisted chain

Two versions of twisted chain are given. Work with 3 or 4 ply yarn and 2.50mm or 3.00mm hook.

For both versions join yarn in first st of row, inserting hook under both loops at top of "ridge", dc in first st, *4ch, miss next st, dc in next st, 4ch... proceed as Version 1 or 2.

Version 1 ("beaded" effect)

Pass hook in front of both short lengths of ch and, holding these to the back, insert hook into the missed st from the back, dc in missed st. Rep from * to end.

Version 2 ("Coiled scroll" effect) Bring hook towards you under both short lengths of ch and insert in missed st from front, dc in missed st. Rep from * to end.

3. Scallop Loop - ss and ch

Using 3 or 4 ply yarn with 2.50 or 3.00mm hook, and working under one loop only of each st along the "ridge", *1ss 3ch 1ss in same st, rep from * to end of row.

2 rows of scallop loop lying close together side by side on the same "ridge" produces evenly "wiggly" lines. These can be interrupted here and there with small bobbles in contrasting colour.

4. Small Bobbles

*1ss 3ch 1dtr 1ss in same st, 1ss in next st, or in each of next 2 or 3sts, rep from * as many times as desired.

While it is possible to use many types of edging st, such as crab st or picot along the "ridges" they may prove too dense or heavy and the "ridge" itself will not lie straight and true after working. It is usually more satisfactory to use combinations of ch and ss - selecting a variant which best suits and displays the yarn in use. For example, with certain fancy boucle yarns try the following: 1ss in first st, * work a length of ch equal in length to the next 4 or 5sts along the ridge, miss these sts, 1ss in next st along the "ridge", rep from * as required.

5. Loop st or Fur st [when cut]

This can be used when the "ridges" run horizontally and are quite widely spaced, eg on a background of tr or dtr raised at the front on every row. Providing the loops are properly secured they can be cut to form a fringe. Could be effective for shawls, stoles or capes.

Large motifs which can be sewn on afterwards

In all the examples given it is the choice of yarn which is important.

1. Ox-eye daisies (Marguerites)

Centre: I used one strand soft, lightweight mohair (Sofil - grey-green) together with one strand of fine unbrushed mohair (yellow). This was to give the impression of pollen on anthers.

Method: Wind the 2 yarns tightly round forefinger 12 times, remove this "ring" from finger and insert 5.00mm hook through centre from front to back, draw yarns through from behind, 1ch, * work 8dc into ring ss to first st to join, rep from * once. The back is the RS because it is raised and well padded. Do not turn before working petals.

Petals: These are worked only part way round centre in most cases (about 5 petals), to give a sense of perspective.

With WS facing and using a lightweight mohair in cream or white ss to any dc of centre, * 5ch, 3 long open tr, yoh, draw through 4 loops, 5ch, 1ss in same dc, 1ss in next dc, rep from * about 4 times (5 petals worked) ending with 1ss in same dc as beg of last petal.

Buds and backs of daisies: Using green DK and 3.50mm hook 4ch, join with ss to form ring, 5ch, 15 trtr in centre, ss to ch to join. Finish off.

3ch, join to form ring,

Rnd 1: 3ch, 12tr in ring, 2ch.

Rnd 2: 1RtrF in every st to end, ss to join.

With petal colour work as many petals as required in "ridge" formed by Rtr at back.

Work 2 rounds dc on rnd 2 to form a cup shape. Firmly fill your cup and gather up sts of last dc round as for a button.

Stalk:

Work as many ch as you want for length of stalk, ss into every ch. Sew stalk at back of "button" where it is drawn up. Thread free end of stalk through centre of trtr "cup" and draw "button" into "cup". Sew both sections together just behind petals.

2. "Flowering Grasses" with Clones Knots

Choose mohair or brushed wool and a 5.00mm hook.

Work a short length of ch. [5-10ch work satisfactorily]. Hold ch bet thumb and first finger of left hand, *pass hook away from you under the ch and pick up loop from supply thread, pass hook away from you over the ch and pick up loop from supply thread. Rep from * 18 or 19 times, yoh, draw thread through all loops on hook. Draw up tightly and ss in ch just behind the looped knot.

Make another ch and repeat knot as many times as required.

Practice is needed to keep the loops nicely loose and very even.

3. PRIMROSES

Materials: 4 ply yarn in primrose yellow; very small quantity of 4 ply in darker yellow for "pin" (long stigma); 4 ply or DK in soft green for stalk and sepals; 2.00mm hook.

Petals: With primrose yellow yarn make 5ch, 5dtr in first of 5ch, 4ch, turn.

Row 2: 2dtr in first st, 4ch, 1ss in first st, *1ss in next st, 4ch, 2dtr, 4ch, 1ss in same st, rep from * 3 times. Finish off.

Sepals: With pale green make 4ch, 5tr in first of 4ch, 4ch, turn.

Row 2: 1dtr in first st, 4ch, 1ss in same st, *ss in next st, 4ch 1dtr 4ch 1ss in same st, rep from * 3 times. Finish off.

Stalk and stigma

Stalk: With pale green make 7ch, ss in 3rd ch from hook and in each rem ch. Finish off.

Stigma: Wuth dark yellow ss under 2ch at top of stalk, 6ch, ss in 2nd ch from hook and in each ch to end. Finish off, disposing neatly and invisibly of all ends of yellow.

To make up

Hold the petals with the WS of dtr sts towards you (they will then curve outwards in finished flower). Thread the stalk through the ch in which the 5dtr of Row 1 of petals were worked, draw through gently until the stigma lies on one side of the ch and the stalk on the other. Hold the sepals with the RS of dtr sts of Row 2 towards you (they will then curve inwards towards the petals in the finished flower), thread the stalk through the ch in which tr sts of Row 1 where worked. Thread tapestry needle with left over end of pale yellow and sew stitches up first ch and last dtr of Row 1 of petals as far as Row 2 and the 5 separate petals catching in the base of the stigma with first (or last st). Sew up first and last sts of Row 1 of sepals in same way. Finish off securely so all parts are held in correct position.

4. PRIMROSE BUDS

Make stalk as for flower but do not make stigma. With pale yellow ss under 2ch at top of stalk, 4ch 1tr in same place, 5 times, 4ch, turn. Work unfinished dtr in each of 5tr, yrh and draw through all six loops on hook, cut thread leaving sufficient length of yarn to sew first st to last sts of both Rows 1 and 2 to form a "tube" representing the pointed bud. Finish off top of stalk. Make sepals as for flower. Thread stalk through base ch of sepals and sew as in flower.

BUTTONS

Simple Buttons

Using DK with 2.50mm hook, make 3ch, ss in first ch to join in ring.

Rnd 1: (RS) 2ch, 9htr in ring, ss to join, 1ch but do not turn.

Rnd 2: (RS) 1dc in back loop only of every st, ss to first ch to join, 1ch, turn.

Rnd 3: (WS) dc to end, ss to first ch to join. Finish off leaving end about 20cm (8") long.

Thread long end in tapestry needle and weave through top of each st of rnd 3, going under one or both loops at the head of each st as desired. Draw up very slightly to from "cup".

To Fill: Wind a very tight hard little ball of same yarn until it is almost the same size as the "cup". Insert the ball in cup, draw up thread tightly and sew securely. Leave remaining end of thread to sew button in place [corresponding to button-hole].

Little Flower Buttons (As for Apple Blossom)

Materials: 4 ply yarn in 3 colours:

A - green, B - orange and C - cream;

1.75mm and 2.00mm hooks.

To make: With A and 1.75mm hook 3ch, making sure first ch is small.

Rnd 1: 8htr in first ch, ss to top of starting ch. Finish off A.

Rnd 2: Join B in front loop of first htr, 3ch, 1ss in front loop of each htr to end, finish with ss in same loop that B was joined into. Finish off B.

Rnd 3: Change to 2.00mm hook and join C in central loop of first htr, *ss in central loop of next htr, 4ch, rep from * to end ss in same loop that C was joined into. Finish off C.

Rnd 4: Change to 1.75mm hook and A to back loop of first htr, 1ch, 1dc in back [horizontal] loop of each htr. [9sts].

Rnd 5: 1ch, dc to end. Finish off leaving a long end. Thread this end into a tapestry needle and gather through tops of dc. Draw up firmly, covering all ends which serve as stuffing for button base. Stitch securely.

INTERNATIONAL SYMBOLS.

ABBREVIATIONS:

beg begin(ning)

bet between

○ **ch** chain

cm centimetre

cont continue

+ **dc** double crochet

dec decrease

DK double knitting

丰 **dtr** double treble

g gramme

gr group

inc increase

lp(s) loop(s)

mm millimetre

patt pattern

quadtr quadruple treble

Rdtr raised double treble

rem remaining

Rquadtr raised quadruple treble

RS right side

Rtr raised treble

RtrB raised treble back

[pushing stems to back]

RtrF raised treble front *[pushing stems to front]*

Rtrtr raised triple treble

sp space

ss slip stitch

⌒ **st(s)** stitch(es)

tog together

丅 **tr** treble

tr2tog decrease 1tr over 2sts

丰 **trtr** triple treble

WS wrong side

yoh yarn over hook

BIBLIOGRAPHY

Phillips Roger
"Grasses, Ferns, Mosses and Lichens of Great Britain and Ireland"
[Pan] 1980.

Turner Pauline
"Creative Guide to Crochet"
[Batsford] 1983.

Turner Pauline
"The Technique of Crochet"
[Batsford] 1987.

Turner Pauline
"Begin with Creative World of Crochet"
[Crochet Design] 1991.

Walters James
"Crochet Workshop"
[Sidgwick and Jackson Ltd.]
1979.
Revised edition
"New Crochet Workshop"
[in six parts]
[Crochet Design] 1992-93.

Colour Plates

<u>List of photographs</u>

Plate 1 Snowflakes in Summer
         Owl and Flowers Coat (front and back)

Plate 2 Summer Meadow
         Marguerites

Plate 3 Kathleen Basford's Irises
         The original postcard of Monet's Irises

Plate 4 Rouen Cathedral: Harmonie brune (after Monet)

Plate 5 Mossy Wall The Changing Light (Morning/Evening)

Plate 6 Liverworts and Mosses

Plate 7 Fast Train to Fritzler (front and back)

Plate 8 Lichens (front and back)
         Larches and Lichens (front and back)

ACKNOWLEDGEMENTS

Appeal of Crochet first published in September 1992 by Crochet Design 17 Poulton Square, Morecambe LA4 5PZ.

Copyright C **Kathleen Basford** and **Pauline Turner.**

Photographs: **Howard Barlow** and **Pauline Turner.**
Models: **Catherine Verrill: Helena Verrill: Tracy McMinn.**

Graphic Design, Typography and Computer Setting:
Mark Bushell. (tel 061 860 5075)
Andi Chapple. (tel 061 737 1887)

Print Production: **Print Pulse** (tel 061 223 4700)

ISBN 1 874080 95 X

Crochet Design would like to thank the **National Gallery** for their permission to reproduce Monet's Irises within the colour plates of this book.

SOURCES

Woolshop mentioned in "Snow in Summer":
Webster's, 23 Southam Road, Dunchurch,
Nr Rugby (tel 0778 - 816008)

Hooks, Books, etc:
Crochet Design, 17 Poulton Square, Morecambe
LA4 5PZ (tel 0524 831 752)